In The Same Place

A Morning Room

In The Same Place

Poems of Place

N. Thomas Johnson-Medland

Photos by Richard Lewis

RESOURCE *Publications* · Eugene, Oregon

IN THE SAME PLACE
Poems of Place

Copyright © 2016 N. Thomas Johnson-Medland. All rights reserved. Except for brief quotations in critical publications or reviews, no part of this book may be reproduced in any manner without prior written permission from the publisher. Write: Permissions, Wipf and Stock Publishers, 199 W. 8th Ave., Suite 3, Eugene, OR 97401.

Resource Publications
An Imprint of Wipf and Stock Publishers
199 W. 8th Ave., Suite 3
Eugene, OR 97401

www.wipfandstock.com

PAPERBACK ISBN 13: 978-1-4982-8103-4
HARDCOVER ISBN 13: 978-1-4982-8105-8

Manufactured in the U.S.A.   03/23/2016

This volume is devoted to all them that have learned to love place; to them that have sat still long enough to notice themselves outside of themselves.

And, for Christina and Redmond on the occasion of their marriage. Many blessings!

—Tom

"We spend our whole lives in the same place and never leave…"
CHARLES WRIGHT, "RETURNED TO THE YAAK CABIN,
I OVERHEARD AN OLD GREEK SONG," IN APPALACHIA

"Poetry is the kind of thing you have to see from the corner of your eye. You can be too well prepared for poetry. A conscientious interest in it is worse than no interest at all, as I believe Frost used to say. It's like a very faint star. If you look straight at it you can't see it, but if you look a little to one side it is there.

"If people around you are in favor, that helps poetry to be, to exist. It disappears under disfavor. There are things you know, human things, that depend on commitment; poetry is one of those things. If you analyze it away, it's gone. It would be like boiling a watch to see what makes it tick."

WILLIAM STAFFORD
WRITING THE AUSTRALIAN CRAWL

Contents

Introduction | ix

The Poems

Among the Ivory and Lavender | 3
If A Stone | 5
Beautiful Land | 7
Standing Firm | 11
Place | 14
It Is Here | 18
I Hear The Wasp | 21
Suspend The Tears | 23
Our Lives are Brindled Feeling | 26
How Can This Place | 30
Lay the Words Out | 33
A Settling Mist | 38
Eyes of Time | 41
Clambering Toward The Silence | 48
They Watch For It In Your Eyes | 52
Passages Behind the Heart | 58
Here | 63
The Priests of Nemi | 65
The Proximity of Alchemy | 69
That Spot By The Tall Oak | 77
That Old Maxwell House Can | 81
When This Place Becomes Everywhere | 82
The Pre-Rain Air | 84

Mincing Words with Whitman
Poems Written at the Grave of Our Native Son in Camden, NJ

This Rock Of My Reflection | 93

Sharing The Dirt | 96

Reaching | 97

The Dead | 100

Tanging | 103

Bee-Space | 113

I Speak Gold | 119

Having to Find Myself | 123

The Felling of a Tree | 129

The Time It Takes To Grow A Soul | 136

A Settling Mist | 145

Having to Amble | 148

I Am Not Sure | 151

The Ambivalence Of A Cloud | 154

The Way Of Waiting | 155

I Find It Fitting | 156

The Climate March Poem—A Rant I | 161

The Climate March Poem—A Rant II | 163

The Climate March Poem—A Rant III | 166

From Penn's Sylvan Lands | 169

Upon This Brittle Soil | 175

O Camden, My Camden | 178

Introduction

Sustaining two seemingly opposing ideas at one and the same time is not simply an indicator of the existence of a neo-cortex, it is a keen marker that the thinker is human and a mature human at that. Being able to think locally and non-locally in terms of entities, ideas, states, and such is very high up there on the evolutionary brain scale.

The developed mind and heart and person—for that matter—can be identified by their ability to sustain complexity. As we grow and develop we are able to do more than one thing at a time and this includes thinking, feeling, hoping and performing. It is just a benchmark of growth.

I do not want to venture toward what number of chronologic years and or what psycho-social level (i.e., developmental years) are required as a numeric milestone for what it means to be mature. Primarily, because this is a volume of poems on place and not on neural development or even neural linguistics. A volume of poems concerning place.

Suffice it to say, if you can hold the notion that place has everything to do with meaning, and its opposite—that place has absolutely nothing to do with meaning—as simultaneously possible and true without exclusion, then you could surmise a mature human neo- cortex is your default operating system. And, therefore in kind, if you could hold that meaning has absolutely everything to do with place; and, also that meaning has absolutely nothing to do with place, then blah, blah, blah. . .neo-cortex. . .blah, blah, blah . . .operating system.

That being said, the concept of locale and or where a thing is, has so much to say about what a thing is. If a thing takes place "here," there is some sort of residue of the "hereness" of that thing that has smeared itself onto the surface of that thing's meaning. The same is then true about the "there" in which a thing may have taken place in or not. "Hereness" and 'thereness" impact a thing's "suchness."

Introduction

* * *

There is some real value in finding a locale—a space that we can call the here and now—and fight for it, defend it, and win it over and against all forces that wish to take it and make it "there" or "then." It gives us the chance to call a thing "mine" or "ours." The true mistake; however, would be to not acknowledge that "this too shall pass"; most likely, within the twinkling of an eye. We grasp, we gain, we hold, and we lose.

Things change quickly. When you are very, very close to the center of the change and when you are at a good and healthy distance from the change it may look like the change happens slowly. But, it is purely relative. Because, if you are farther away it looks as if it happens quickly. And, if you are far enough away, it does not even appear that change occurs at all. Such is the mystery of time and place.

So, "here" and "there," "now" and "then" are all ways of expressing place (both in time and space). They all make a difference in how the suchness of a thing is and is perceived. It may be the here and now of the earth or spaces on it, but it might also be the here and now of the interior character of who you are.

Space and time are not just terms and functions of the bigger/larger objects in our lives, but intricately woven into the cells that make up our spleen and the neuro-transmitters that carry our sense of truth and integrity (or some other thing that carries that—which we have not yet figured out how to find or name just yet). The Mercurial and Hermetic principle that everything above operates on similar principals as the things below (inside as well as outside) holds true in this conversation as we might expect.

We impact where we are—in space and in time. Where we are in space and time impacts us as well. From a distance or a different vantage point, none of this seems true. Close up and at other places all of this seems true. This is what we can sustain when we are growing.

All of this being said, I suppose the journey this collection is meant to set us on is the journey of exploration to see how we are woven into and among the where and when of who and what we are. Push and test the connections and the spaces in between to see how the one is or is not showing itself to be the other. Get a sense of what influences and in which direction.

Introduction

* * *

When we go back home we can feel a flood of emotion and suchness that makes us feel as if no time has elapsed. We readily pick up old ideas, notions, beliefs and ways of inhabiting our skin. We feel to be our old self. Likewise, when we set out to new places and times in our lives we take pieces of who we have been into those places and that impacts them.

I think we sense the reality of these ideas in simple ways like how going to the ocean can make us feel different than we do when cooped up in our homes during the snowstorms of winter. Or, we can feel the difference when we stand at the foot of Half-Dome in Yosemite National Park and stare up, as opposed to catching crayfish in the trickle of a stream along the road and under the culvert back home. Place impacts us and we it.

We need to overlay the idea of time on top of this because we can sense changes in the impact of place when we compare them to other times. We have all felt how small and colloquial our childhood home feels when we are grown up and come back to visit after a long time away. We know how returning to places of college experiences we do not always feel the same as we did when we were there before. Times and places seem to be somehow different then we have held them to be in our memory. Place matters. Time matters. Place impacts us and we it. Time impacts us and we it.

But, it is not just that simple. The antithesis is also true. We impact them as well.

There is some corrective sameness about returning home that cools us down and eases our inner disconnection with our sense of self over time. But, we also bring our newness back into that oldness in a way that shapes it as well.

It is odd like that. I get a real strong alchemical sense that our desires themselves somehow shape the way we perceive the places and spaces, the times and the eras of our being and having been in and among them. Like anything else in life, we have the choice to turn base lead into gold, if but we would so choose.

Introduction

* * *

In common, less abstract terms, it matters where and when you grow up. It somehow impacts you. And, from a different place—perhaps further away in time and space—it really looks as if it has no impact. You have changed as you move further away in time and space. Both seem true.

I think of the number of times that walking in the woods helped me calm and soothe my inner anguish and angst. It has always been a place of peace and awe for me. That feeling has built up enough over time so I may go to the woods anytime and it will help me settle and find my core. Always. This speaks to the amount of meaning I have allowed the wilds to have for me and the amount of meaning I have allowed my me to add to being in the wilds. It is reciprocal.

And, perhaps that is what place and its corollary time really beg from us. A collaboration. Place and time impact us and we them. We are called and call them to interact with us and we them. Place (and therefore time) weave themselves into us and we them. This mingling and cohabitation allows for residues of each and the other to hunger and call for each other when they are together and even more so apart.

The little pieces of hometown, or of bitter anguish from a hard life call to us like magnets. Always seeking to attract more of what we had so we may feel whole and at ease again. And too, we are sometimes pulled toward the opposite—a simple recoiling against the harshness of what we knew and have now come to call dark matter in our lives.

Pushed and pulled by time and space, we will never find our meaning in who we have become unless we are able to determine if it is the time and space that calls us to them or pushes us away from them. Called because of the fondness; repelled because of the shame. But, called and repelled, none the less.

So, I guess I am back at the place where I started more or less.

Place (and therefore time) matters. It shapes us and impacts us and we it. Figuring out how it shapes and is shaped is what we spend our days learning about ourselves and our environs—whether we pay attention and understand it or not.

We have a neo-cortex to help us sort through the complexity and the layered shading of these ideas and notions, using the dappled sense of meaning to survive beyond what we would have without a neo-cortex. It helps us hold similar and opposite things in contention at the same time—seeking a balance and synthesis.

And then there is this. All of what I have said above operates for stages and states in our lives as well (sort of the inner versions of space and time).

I like the sense of place that comes from identity. Let's say: I am in a peaceful place right now—at this point in my life. This portion of the journey is settled and calm. My life is luxuriantly at rest. Then I hit a bump and end up in a situation that is agitating and unruly. I become restless and anxious.

I can stand where I am at this point in my life—in a portion of life that is good, and experience a ripple on the surface of that place. I can hold opposites within.

I love this part of life—the way an inner space can become a place from which to journey from. These notions are really place, but not necessarily a spot to set up a chair and hang out. We may live in these places or in and out of them, but they inhabit us and we them in the same way we do a cave or a Highland's vista. And, time—particularly felt as duration in these instances—is clearly woven into the inner landscapes.

"Over there" is about hope. "Over there" allows us to dream. "Right here" is what we've got. "Right here" is as it is now.

Seeing those places in the hillside, or on the beach, or along the river brings possibility. They are far enough away that we can believe life would be different there—we would be different there. So, there is a lot of therapy bound up in far off and future spaces, places, and times. We have the distance to imagine difference.

Bringing "that" and "this" together is our landscape. We knead these differences into our poems to reveal truth. We sprinkle our pile of words with "what is" and "what could be" so people can make sense of here and there. Place unfolds in meaning as words are given to describe its texture and depth. Without words we would be lost for understanding and design. We could not craft brave new worlds out of what we have in front of us—what we find pleasant.

And so, it is not just the place of place that is vital and integral to human health, and growth, and homeostasis. It is the words we give to describe and assign meaning to place that also bear out much of the import of place and space.

How we hold place and how we hope to mold space is tied up in our sense of here and there; of now and then. We define places in our lives and

Introduction

are defined by places in our lives. As with all the rest of life, place lives on the razor's edge; somewhere betwixt and between the duality of oneness and the conjunction of opposing forces. Having full and rich meaning all its own; and only being what it is believed to be by each.

How some thing in us reaches out through our whole; and, connects with all that is on the horizon is a determined search we set ourselves out on—all of our days. Often we do not know we are venturing. The mystery of that place and this, keep us ever pushing onward to find a resolution to some deeply hidden question that lurks in the recesses of our "me." The question about identity. And, since identity is always happening in space and in time, it seeks to know the worth of them as well. Am I that? Is that me? Is there correlation? Does now, or then have sway on me?

These are the genuine human tools that seek to aid us in finding consciousness and "I-ness" in our short journey on this dirt. These poems try a bit to figure all of this out. They are yours.

The Poems

Among the Ivory and Lavender

In the abundance of
heavy fogged moisture

lay the overwhelming smell
of verbena and phlox.

The very air
scintillating and
alive with the ivory
and lavender hues

hidden behind
a floral aroma—
a tapestry

for the nose.

The road winds through
this place—these
places—

along the river towns
of Pennsylvania—

building up the
storehouse of pleasantries
from the onslaught of Spring.

Spring,

it creeps itself
into this
place slowly;

In The Same Place

moving ever on
through the mountains'
alluviations and
foothills. Seeking
to inhabit the
higher places of the
river valley.

This plague of
color and
deviation
from dirt
and
bark

smites the crenulations of
these crenelated
places each year.

For, this sickness;

for,
this cancerous
ravishing force of greening
newness and the bud

I shall find a deep
seated thanks
and

praise for this.

This is
where
I am
transformed.

If A Stone

If a stone should
fall out from the bottom;

fall out from the middle
of the bottom
of a wall
along the
boundary of a field;

would that change things?

Would time
fall through the stones
into the dirt
and somehow
wash away important things
that we had only just
remembered from our past.

Things we swore
as children

we would never regress upon—
never undo our
severity of emotion
and belief for.

Or, would it just be
a break in the bottom
of a stone wall
that runs along a field

at the base

In The Same Place

of a red shale mountain
just outside Uhlerstown,
Pennsylvania.

At the end of spring,
I believe.

Beautiful Land

Only give me some
space—be it ever so small—

to lay my head and ponder.

Only give me some
space—be it ever so tiny—

to sit myself and stare.

The place
where one piece of land
meets another—

ALMOST.

The space
where one mountain
reaches itself down and out

toward the upward slope of another—

ALMOST.

There is a river
there that runs between
the betweens of that
place.

There is an echo
there that bounces
off the mountain walls.

In The Same Place

It is in that great space
of the between
you tilled the earthy
loam of compassion.

It is in that expansive place
of the echo
you planted tender
seedlings of giving.

The purpling shadows
of the dawn-rise mist
drape the moistening
soil and feed the
youngling trees.

The days will wear on
and it will not be long
before the trees you
have nursed offer
sheltering shade and
generative seed.

Ponder and stare

- with me—

upon the grove
you have planted;

blossom and leaf
are soon to bud.

Come into this
valley of tenderness

and gentle giving;

find repose
among the spreading
limbs and cold running
water.

This place is of your
own creating.

This space is of your
own design.

This is where you
shall find your "you."

Only give me some
space—be it ever so small—

to lay my head and ponder.

Only give me some
space—be it ever so tiny—

to sit myself and stare.

The place
where one piece of land
meets another—

ALMOST.

The space
where one mountain
reaches itself down and out

toward the upward slope of another—

ALMOST.

In The Same Place

There is a river
there that runs between
the betweens of that
place.

There is an echo
there that bounces
off the mountain walls.

This beauty is yours;
this beauty is

you.

Standing Firm

Standing firm
and facing into
the edges of these hills

into the edges
of those valleys

and
the river

out along
the far reaches;

I am able
to slow enough
to hear

only the wind
dancing

with the
leaves and tiny
branches

of the trees.

I can hear
an underlying
melody cascading
up and out of

the Delaware

In The Same Place

as it courses
with power through
the red shale Gap.

It is from this place,
it is in that melody
I hear the subtle
variations that
my heart has learned
to long for.

A melody that sings
to me of beehives
and of doves;

of loamy
woodland trails
and knolls.

It is here I have
learned to sing of
what a man is when
there is no movement out
and away from the center.

Sloping Appalachians,
rising up among the
foothills of my youth;

you have consumed me
and left me
mesmerized
by the shrill trill
of your insects
and birds,
of your tree frogs
and raccoons.

Standing Firm

I am lost
in a cacophony
that has destroyed
the mayhem of

civilized existence.
It is gone.

Place

Place is the
kind of thing
that gets under
the nails, behind
the ears, and
between the toes.
It follows you
everywhere—
lending just a
hint of displacement
and yearning toward
the sun of home—

a flower turning
to the solar path;
all day long.

You can almost
hear it in every
sound; just enough
to know that this
new space is not
"IT."

Dorothy took
it with her and
used "IT" as a beacon
to escape the wonders
of Oz.

Moses had "IT"
just behind his eyes
so he could know the

Place

place he had only
dreamed of.

Indians and
dinosaurs longed
for "IT" before they
died and would
walk an aimless
outward journey
by feeling an
inner trek to the
place that was
the origin of their
very own self.

Columbus
set out to
find the
place of his
discovery
hoping it would
mirror the "IT"
of what he
knew—

amplified with
untold riches.

You get older
and the longing
for the remnants
of place grows
deeper, richer, and
stronger with each
passing moist
breath of
time apart.

In The Same Place

The skin can
feel "IT" in an
instant, the nose
knows "IT" with
one whiff.

We search our days
for similar warmth and
familiar tastes; a fireside
seat and the hint of
cinnamon and clove.

The sun can
slant itself
in just the same
way; the air can
blow itself in
a long known
fashion. That
then becomes
"IT" and we
have arrived.

What is our life
but an ongoing
and defiant shaping
of all that is
into all that
used to be.
This is
where the
old can touch the
new; the
past can
change our
future.

Place

We begin ourselves in
a place called home;
a place that
has made all the difference.
It gave us
the lexicon of
being that we carried
and used the remainder
of our days
to make sense
of all that is.

Place is the
kind of thing
that gets under
the nails, behind
the ears, and
between the toes.
It follows you
everywhere—
lending just a
hint of displacement
and yearning toward
the sun of home—

a flower turning
to the solar path;
all day long.

It Is Here

It is here
that the flatter lands
and ambling slopes
turn upward toward
the sky. A red shale
mountain along the
edges of the mountains;
an inkling of rocks
climbing out of the earth.
A true foothill
of and in its own right.

There is a stark
and yet subtle rise
at just this place
along the river where
the Green Hill and
River Roads meet.

Each day I pass this
spot there is a feeling
in the center of my me
that says, "This is
where one place becomes
another. This is the place
of uniqueness among a somewhat
feeling flatland of sameness
in life and degree."

It excites the soul
to notice such things.
Delight floods the heart
directly from the sensibility

and collaboration grown
from the mixed arrangement
of the eyes and mind.

Beauty is born by an
inner capturing of the visible
disturbance in the line of
sight somehow translated
to mean something beyond just
that thing it holds in view.

From this point forward
the foothills show off their
rivuleted alluviations that
sing toward the earth from
their peaks just beyond the
tall pines. Small mountain falls
burst forth in the melting of the
snows to reveal a spring that
would remain unnoticed on most
days—hidden under leaf and
limb, invisible to the eye and heart.

Softly the earth pads
on, rising until it peaks itself
in a summit along the
Alleghenies. How can you not
walk the earth and feel
the hidden innuendo of
tribes and shamans making
offerings to the crafter
of this place. How can
you fail to sense the
fact of a holler and the
truth of a
primordial grove of mountain
laurel it conceals from
the faint. Rare moments are

In The Same Place

everywhere to be seen
by the feeling of the heart
in the ever-present space
its feet tread upon.

It is here
that the flatter lands
and ambling slopes
turn upward toward
the sky. A red shale
mountain along the
edges of the mountains;
an inkling of rocks
climbing out of the earth.
A true foothill
of and in its own right.

It is here,
right here
where I stand
upon this earth
on my own two feet.
Leaving my car
just along the side of
the road so my heart
could sing.

Here.

I Hear The Wasp

I hear the wasp
at the front door;
banging into
the screen again,
and again, and again.
It is as if its wings
have lost touch with
its brain and cannot
know that it should stop.
I saw this once
in a squirrel that insisted
the glass of the door did
not exist. It ran against
the surface and bounced off
four times before
it somehow reckoned
defeat. There is an
irony in the depth of
these things we
hear and see when
we are alone. It rings
somehow differently than
those same things are
known with another. The
laughter is somehow more
personal; like the nest I know
this wasp longs to daub.

I heard that
line about the screen
door from Bly while
at the Waterloo Village.

In The Same Place

It was his but it
now has become mine;
and in that robbing
of words and images
I have made that place
come to bear on this place.

His was about a
moth, I believe.

I heard it in my
son's singing voice
last night. It was mine.
Only I sang that song
in the seventh grade
with Kenny Lanzetta as
we swore his uncle was
going to record us
and somehow make us
BIG.

This place now shares
some of that.

Suspend The Tears

(for Elaine and Sharon)

This purpling-grey
mountain holler
suspends the tears
the chill night sky
could find no way
to shed. The tears
she held as memory
of you.

This holler will
bloom in crocus.

These rising foothills
of greening life weep
in an endless knowing
that she has slipped
on by—gone.

Lost, the gentle
touch of tenderness
and grace. A lily in
this valley of life and
its constant everyday
living.

This good earth
has been opened
endlessly for our
gathering of minerals
and warmth. It is
this day that we return

In The Same Place

a gem that shines both
here as always in
the far and beyond.

Look kindly into
the Mystery for us;
look deeply into the Light.
We turn to speak
but find you gone;
we lean to listen
but you've gone home.

For, Osie,
O, dear Osie,
for a while
we will lose our way.

Our weary feet will
firm with passing;
our sorrowed hearts
will fill.

This purpling-grey
mountain holler suspends
the tears the chill night
sky could find no way
to shed. The tears she held
as memory of you.

This holler will
bloom in crocus.
These hearts will
bloom in you.

A Quiet Afternoon

Our Lives are Brindled Feeling

(for Lighthouse Hospice Social Workers 2014)

Our lives are brindled
shades of feeling;

our days are
mottled hues of thought.
Cascading over the
epochs of time,
stretching always out
and just beyond the
full measure of our
grasp and sight.

We are unsure of
where the river goes
beyond its turning
bend and wending
way. Spilling its
purpling muddy
courses onward.

We cannot know what
wind will blow just
up ahead; we cannot say
what lies in wait
at the noonday. A blast of
heat or tempest
on our face.

We can only
learn to say
how we will hold ourselves

against all that comes at us;

how we will hold ourselves
within all we will yet be glad
to know.

The rose petals
lie still
in their own
aging beauty,
fading slowly over time.

The eyes see
only this;
brittle flower flesh,
dried and gathering
the dust of death.

The heart adds
vibrant layers
to what is seen:

meaning from that day,
feeling for that "one,"

a scent upon the air,
a flutter on the skin
a swirling mass of
intuition and repose.

A cavalcade of days—when
love shared love
with love and marked its
passing with flower,
stem and leaf.

Our memory holds
them fresh for just

In The Same Place

only so long—a rough
ceramic bowl of our own
collecting. The heart
it knows another way.

Gently walk them
to the edge of the garden;

silently show them
the footfall's echo.
They will turn for you
and you will be gone,
your touch a distant
sense among it all.

Our lives are brindled
shades of feeling;

our days are
mottled hues of thought.
Cascading over the
epochs of time,
stretching always out
and just beyond the
full measure of our
grasp and sight.

We are unsure of
where the river goes
beyond its turning
bend and wending
way.

We cannot know what
wind will blow just
up ahead; we cannot say
what lies in wait
at the noonday.

Our Lives are Brindled Feeling

We can only learn to say
how we will hold ourselves
against all that comes at us;

how we will hold ourselves
within all we will yet be glad
to know.

How Can This Place

How can this
place, this same
one spot that
carries itself
across the landscape
of extended time
and incremental
turnings of space
hold anything

like meaning and
a sense of indicated
preference.
How is it my
heart stills and
my every cell
relaxes when I
pull into the
treacherously steep
driveway of our home?

Why does the
soul shift toward
calm simply grabbing a
carved oak railing
at their home—
climbing the carpet-less
stairs that echo each
and every footfall
up the center of the
stairwell of three floors?

When did the niche

of moss covered rock,
along the waterfall of
that stream weld itself
to homeostasis;
and, give shear release
of tension gathered
under the skin and the
follicles of every strand
of hair?

The Pleiades
could better stand
a chance at answer
than I. The Ocean
could more readily
explain return.

I do not find the
wherewithal
to suppose I could
speak such
mystery and mirth.

I can lean a bit
into the bliss of locale
by learning to sense
what way the places
I inhabit leave me
to feel. It is there

I can steady my
gaze into the
chasm of the
eternal fields that
occupy each atom;
and align myself
with the
universe of all

In The Same Place

arisings that
live in every
here—

along the axis
of all our

nows.

Lay the Words Out

(for the Support Staff of Lighthouse Hospice 2014)

The day hangs
on the tone
of your voice,

on the way you
lay the words out
for them to amble
gently
across
into
this new sunrise.

This path
pulls at the corners
of their mouth—

a smile joins
the lineaments of
their despair to
rest.

How the wind
dies down and
leaves a calm across
the surface of the lake
speaks endless tomes
to the arrival of
unbridled relief
from the milk of
human kindness.

In The Same Place

Gentleness attends
the simple flow of
rainwater along
the way.

Rivulets course attentive
to escape. Where
to find a small
break in the icy
banks of snow?

Looking for one chance
toward freedom. To leave
the confines of myopic
isolation and join
the mighty river.

How they wish
to be away from
this their countless
hours of singular
journey and closure
with no words. What
hand will throw them
the rope of steady return

to the constant
chatter of human
shoulders rubbing
at their side—drawing
them to the
endless distraction
of the mundane
and plain old,
plain old.

This loneliness
of the mountain pass

can only be replaced
by wonder when

we feel safe on our
little piece of earth—
the one upon
which we stand.

Perched and nestled
in a place of comforting
ease, we can turn our
eyes to the mighty
torrents and know the
song "that all shall
be well" as more
than just

a lilting and lifeless
refrain, but
the true hymn
of the Cosmos.

The day hangs
on the tone
of your voice,

on the way you
lay the words out
for them to amble
gently
across
into
this new sunrise.

This path
pulls at the corners
of their mouth—

In The Same Place

a smile joins
the lineaments of
their despair to
rest.

How the wind
dies down and
leaves a calm across
the surface of the lake
speaks endless tomes
to the arrival of
unbridled relief
from the milk of
human kindness.

Gentleness attends
the simple flow of
rainwater along
the way.

Rivulets course attentive
to escape. Where
to find a small
break in the icy
banks of snow?

Looking for one chance
toward freedom. To leave
the confines of myopic
isolation and join
the mighty river.

An Evening in New Hope

A Settling Mist

(for Glinda, Zachary, Josiah)

Outside—
a settling mist
falls so familiar
and so fair.

It is an imperceptible
blanket of content
morning rapture and
warm glow release
that holds me in

this place as if
melted in my own
bed at home—with
Glinda; the boys
moving slowly
in their rooms
to greet the day.

It is here—
with a book
of simple words
and a cup of
coffee—I am
able to bring that
outside air and
bliss inside myself
to grow.

A Settling Mist

It is a full surround
gift of words and
notions—

slowly
trickling over the
rocks of mystery
and manner that
pulsate out from
the timeless beyond
and back.

This day
holds no special
claim on the life
that moves within
this sack of cells;

it is the scintillating
strand of poetry
that impresses itself
in me and back—

always back—
through time to

all their hearts
and pens. It is not
just Bly, and Hass,
Shihab-Nye, Snyder,
and Stafford
that glow; it is Frost

and Whitman, Shelley,
and Satho, Basho,
and Issa—the

whole damned lineage

In The Same Place

of word craft sorters
and impression laced
builders that shatter my
isolation with light.

Light creeps in slowly
and replaces my me
with a they that falls
lusciously over the

rocks of time and
sings a melody of
infinite meaning and
a camaraderie of
of all that unites

us beyond our skin.

Eyes of Time

How is this land
laid out across the
boundary of my days?
Can my mid-life
eye match
itself to the
heart I grew
throughout my living?
Where is the grave
of mom-mom and pop-pop?

Each tree feels
like "the tree"

by their place
of rest
on this soil
of their repose.
The strange
familiar is shadowed
and replaced
by doubts and
ambling that
betrays a need
to find what I
think I should
be able to know.

I wander
and can
feel my eyes crying out
to my heart
for some

In The Same Place

inkling of impression,
some remembrance
of the way the leaves
of grass
had once leaned
this way and that
into the place of their
still bodies.

I hear his voice
mocking
my childhood hair
that had grown
beyond the edges
of his comfort.

He told me
he would find
a yellow ribbon
for my locks,
which makes me
laugh today—

because—
as by chance—
I have
pulled my hair
back—to a ponytail—
and secured it
with the only hairband
in my car—yellow.
The circuitousness of
my days brings a
chuckle enjoyment to
my being.

Still, I cannot
find the place they have

Eyes of Time

lain in the ground
these many years.

Odd, the tricks
time plays on the
thing we hold to
so very dear.

Looking for familiar,
we find a harrowing
newness revealed in
ways that cannot allow us
a moment of wonder.
What is to become
of the heart that
longs for remembrance
and finds only strangeness
all around.

The dappled light of a
tree against a cloudless
sky somehow catches
my eye for just
one slivered instant
of a quickly
passing second;

and my feet
remember the path
to their grave in ways
my heart finds astounding.

There they are.

Their bronze marker
covered in layers
of dried silt and dead
roots. Their silent dismay

In The Same Place

at the lack of care asks
me why I have not come
to them before.

I sit there
with them and
eat my lunch.
Can they hear
the words I share
with them about
what I do and who
I have become in
the absence of their
living at my side?

My bee brush
is a worthy friend to
help me clean the
dirt from the memory
of the metal plate that
slowly reveals their
names to me and
the numbers of their
days on this earth-place.

As the memories
tumble slowly from
my mind onto the empty
lines of the journal in
my car, I am transfixed
by the power that
letters can have
to help recall a life
to the mind
and to the heart.

And, on this day,
as I sit here composing

Eyes of Time

words of that day of
discovered tales and
colored impressions
from my youth, I look
for the book that is
no longer here—
at my side—to give
me direction along the
lineaments of their lives
and order the things
I felt sitting there in
that day's sun
of simple repose.

Again, there is no
magic harbinger of the
then in the now. A leaf
falls to the ground but once
and dies a thousands days
as it becomes the earth
upon which we stand.

Can my mid-life
eye match
itself to the
heart I grew
throughout my living?
What I know
for sure,
is the bronze was
clean and
their memory
strong for just one
moment on the underside
of the winds of remembering.
The glint of a forgotten
path revealed itself
across a few

In The Same Place

small increments
of this rival we call

time.

Birches

Clambering Toward The Silence

I found
a very small
piece
of myself
clambering
toward the silence
at the edges
of life—
out
along the places
where desolation
has come to be
the lay
of the land.

There should
have been
no one there;
and yet,
it was
strewn all
about with bodies
and heaps of decay.
Who knew?

I came here to
lament the lunacy
of the city—

the madness of
the dwellers of
concrete and macadam.

Clambering Toward The Silence

They have taken
to passing a motion;
taken to passing
an unbridled act
of desperation.
An act of greed,
and of planning,
and of drilling,
and of blasting away
along the
edges of my Delaware—

among the basin of
our River and of
our very future and
the future of our Sister
Water.

She winds her way
along, and through
and among the land
and the villages that
have nestled themselves
on her banks
for countless ages—

Ages Unto Ages.

The echoes of the
thousand, thousand
voices
of time
carry themselves
across
her surface,
across
her skin,
across

In The Same Place

the flesh
feeling ripples of her
dank and aroma'd shores.
First, mud,
then fish,
then shell,
then weed,
then mud, again.

Oh, my sick and
sordid love
of this ambient measure
of what it means to
be a man could soon
come to an end.
Would that others
would speak their
affair with
the earth, with
the rivers, with
the sky herself.
But, no. In the
place where silence
should tender the
art of wooing enamor-ment
it stands instead against
the affair of the soul
with matter.

What man shall stand,
what woman proclaim
the madness of greed
for more? In the end,
it shall all
be undone.

Time and the
whirling passage

of its core of
ebbing upheaval
will break apart
the matter
of who we are.
Barons will be
given to entropy
and decay as will
the pen, and heart,
and voice of this
unknown poet.

But, oh
the solemn risk we run
of coming to our
falling apart
in a wasteland of
disarray and toxic
calumny exposed.

Would we should
come undone amid
a beauty of resplendent
glee; a bliss we
follow—like a thread—
to the ground from
which we have come.

They Watch For It In Your Eyes

(for Lighthouse Hospice Nurses 2014)

They watch for it—
in your eyes—

the slightest tremor
or wince of dismay.

They see only the bright
boldness that shines
straight out from
your soulful self
holding love;

like a pool of ocean
backwater

along a jetty.

A place for them to
play amid the roughness
of the waves that seem
all so strong.

All around. Your
glance gives peace.

Your eyes—

a mountain stream—

so clear from an ever
flowing spring.

They Watch For It In Your Eyes

Wisdom tears
of the heart
that slake

both sorrows'
and joys'
ever present thirst.

They listen for it
in the clarity
of your message
and the in tone
of your voice.

Unlike others,

you are not afraid
to speak of that which slips
away between the recesses
of the daylight of
their youth—
those things that they
hold onto;
a first kiss,
a child's first steps,
the joy that lit their eyes.

The beauty
of who they have been
is a grace for
their own selves
to remember—

daffodils pushing through
the dark dank layer
of last season's leaves.
The rich

In The Same Place

aroma of hyacinth in
the early morning
mist and heavy dew
calling them to be still.

Your voice
an ever present pool
of safety;
cool and inviting.
Your words
laid out in such a way
to wend them through
their end of time;

bricks

in patterned fashion
through the rosemary
of the mind.

They feel for it
in your touch

that feathers ever so lightly
over the blanket of their skin;

hanging so gingerly
on the body of their dying.

So paper thin and fine;

rescued
from the tattering
and the tears
by the fondness
of your soul
for gentleness

and comfort

slathered
on by layer after
layer of loving care.

The space you tend
with them is worthy
of the dying of a Royal.

Laurel draped upon their
every act, and thought, and word
and whim.

You gesture them on
and tell them
how it is to be
for them as they
move, so elegantly through
the heaviness,

so slowly toward
the dimming of the light.

They watch for it—
in your eyes—

the slightest tremor
or wince of dismay.

They see only the bright
boldness that shines
straight out from
your soulful self
holding love;

In The Same Place

like a pool of ocean
backwater

along a jetty.

A place for them to
play amid the roughness
of the waves that seem
all so strong.

All around. Your
glance gives peace.

Your eyes—

a mountain stream—

so clear from an ever
flowing spring.

Wisdom tears
of the heart
that slake

both sorrows'
and joys'
ever present thirst.

Bromley Mill

Passages Behind the Heart

(for Lighthouse Hospice Pastoral Care Staff 2014)

There are passages,
tender,
wispy trails
and tunnels

just behind the heart.

They hold images,
and thoughts,
and meandering
impressions

that mean so
very much
when we consider
what it is to be
a man;
to be
a woman on this
occasionally desolate
and lonely marble
suspended here in a cosmos
spacious
beyond comprehension.

Small streams of
yesterday feelings,
and trails of rose petals
that have soaked up
so much
of the feeling of

our days on this earth.
Rivulets of apprehension
and adulation linger
in these passages
and
on the stuff that
passes through them.

Many have a luxury
to count this space—
these places—

as lost
or
non-existent.

Not you.

You keep
dear this
treasure-hold
of confused
remembrance
and slippery content
of numbered days.

A man knows
the first time he loved
her and where that
love fell tattered
in disrepair; broken
open in sorrow—
to the ground.

A woman knows
the first time she
felt safe with him
and just when they

In The Same Place

were subjected
to the crumbling
of the walls of protection
and repair.

You hear these tales
as they slowly leak out
from behind the heart;

creeping forth
almost unbeknownst
to the tellers
themselves

You hold them
SACREDLY.

Cool spring water
draughts, cradled in
cupped hands
slake the parched remnants
of what it means
to be human.

How will you give
them back?

How will you
help them to hear
the songs
that drift out
from these spaces
unseen.

These stories lace
themselves up
to gossamer wings.

You set them free
to join the countless
souls of meaning and
repose that
live within a
man;

within a
woman.

A firefly
lights the air;
escaping hands of
mirth and playful
wonder.
It knows
and is known
only as delight.

Find those emissaries of
the heart
that are hidden
in each man;

in each woman
and set
them free,
aloft in the air around
the dying that
we have come to know
as God.

It is that hiddenness,
it is that space,
it is that unleashing
that is the very life of God.
And,
your very place

In The Same Place

on this earth
is
to make sure
the dying do not
miss it
as they leave.

Here

It is seldom
that we arrive
at this place
and call it here;
knowing
it to be
the newness
of the now.

On a precipice
at sunset;
along the coast
at sunrise.
Breathing in
the very essence
of the space on
which we hold our
lives

at that moment
is the feeling
of the hereness
of the here.

We rush
most days
into everything
we do,
life itself
nothing more than
one more deli
or hardware store.

In The Same Place

A death helps
us to see the
here.

A birth helps us
feel the here.

A mystery as
large as
a hummingbird
can shove us into
knowing this place
as if
we had
never been
here
before.

The Priests of Nemi

This is the place
of the destroying
sacrifice, the place
of transmutation
and release.

This is the place
of the slaying god;
and all it calls to
draw forth from
life and the sacredness
of a well-worn
sweetness unreleased.

It is here
that I shall be re-placed
by the one
who shall kill me—

in my own space
made by my own
space of killing—

that
I have perfected in
the wanton desire
of supremacy and
despair. I have
always been about the
task of looking
over my shoulder
for the destroyer

In The Same Place

of myself and my
soul. It is how I took
the throne
of this current
priesthood and kingdom
of power and retribution
for the future of our race.

There shall never be
a ceasing of the over-turning
of the heart. There shall
never come to pass a day
of ending. It shall always be
the rending of the muscle
by the sword; and the soul
shall watch and feel in
supreme and full disgrace.

Nemi, priests of Nemi
I supremely call to thee
and I ask the sacred bounty
of your souls and blood release.

For, the simple act of
dying and the hiding of the
craft shall forever be upon
the species of this feast.

I cannot stop the overlooking
of my shoulder and my back
as I seek to move ahead
within the species of the priest,
but forever I cannot cease the
constant guarding of the heart,
and so forever and forever
I will seek to overcome.

Each day, another

piece of the self comes
to claim the throne
of this auspicious sovereignty
which we shall name

consciousness. And so,
in history and yonder lore
of days gone by, the Priests
of Nemi came to show us
how the constellations
of the self move within.
One mask on the ego
rules this hour, but in the
turning of the hands of time,
another shall be seated on
this same throne. Little constant
is this thing we call here;
ever moving this thing we call now.

What makes up this space; and
what makes up this time?

It is CHANGE; this I have
sung in a thousand, thousand
stanzas of my ode.

That which is
shall be moved.

This here shall
quickly become a "there";
this now
shall soon become a "then."
Move closer to its center
and it slows a bit, but still
from the outer reaches
of this and that all that is
is shifting and becoming

In The Same Place

what it is next to become.
Hold tightly the hands
of the priests of Nemi,
they are everywhere and
in all times. Move yourself
so far away that the gyrations
of this turning evolution are still;
elsewise, hold on for this
eternal ride.

There is no telling
where we shall end;
except,

as above, so below,
as inside so out. The space
where Hermes meets
the priests of Nemi tells more
of this ancient and lurking
tale than we would
care to have suspected.
O sad, modern man, how
have you lost your way?
What psyche of yours
could not gain access to
the universe on the wings
of myth? It is the tales
told round the fire that
have always had the key
to meaning and advance.
For, it is in myth, that we
lay our insides out for
all to see. For all to see.

The Proximity of Alchemy

I have seen
how the snow
perched ever so loosely
on the top
of that branch

of the silver birch
tree

melts its way
down and under
in an instant.

Gone
and now
become.

There, in that space
of constant change
and new becoming
the bark seems
soaked dark
by the trickle of
melt from above.

I have noticed
how sometimes

things so close together

may not be similar
to each other
at all. Their

In The Same Place

relative sameness
is transmuted into
an otherness that
gets lost in
the notion
of utility and ease.

It is our lack
of ingenuity and
clarity of observation
that ruffles our sense
of expectation and ennui.

I have seen
how the river pulls
away everything
that is not
somehow rooted
down or just
heavy enough to
hold its own against
the movement and
the current tides
of shifting light.

What we have hoped for
and expected
is really all about
the sense of need
we have for one
thing to be just like another.

An imagined
stability
that is genuinely
not there.

Nature designs uniqueness

into poles of closeness
and proximity.

A pause
at
the
end
of
a
line
to give
a sense of
understanding and
recline.

I had always thought
that the people of
my hometown had
held a sameness in
the fabric of their
meaning and degree.
But,
I find
that sameness
to be
my need
for nostalgia—

a place
where there is
relative ease, a better
life and a simple
routine.

It is a space
of longing in
all of us
to have a homeland

In The Same Place

and heaven of
hopes. A place
to walk among
the dried and fallen
leaves of our own
imagination. Welcomed.
And, belonging.

And, it is
a conspiring collusion
we all allow
in
order
that
we
may
find a space to
sit and feel at home.

This proximity
to alchemy;
and, the making
of things into
what we
need for them
to be

happens along
the thin line

of desire
and snow
melting
into water
along the edge
of bark on
a winter branch.

The Proximity of Alchemy

For,
how we will
find the world
melting from
snow into water
can only be uncovered
in the seeking place
of yearning hunger.

That leaf,
holding on so long

to the surface
of the ushering brook,

is lost
in an instant

when the rocky shoals of
turbulence
take it
from its throne.

Watch.
Ever-notice
how the shifting
comes
and goes.

It gives out
lessons

all day long
for free
on how to make
the change.

It is yours

In The Same Place

to cross the line
from this place

to that.
What meaning
will it hold?

Does the
melted snow
reach out and long
for the days it stood
atop the branch
as pack?

Do things scattered
here and there by
the rampage and
current crave to
return to the place
from which they
came un-moored?

Is it only
I—the WE of
being human—
that wishes for something
that is not here
and is not now

as if it ALONE
held the magic allure
and deep-seated freedom
of consuming release?

How we wander
looking for riches that
are truly embedded in
the soles of our

The Proximity of Alchemy

shoes;
or, just loosely
trapped
between our feet
and our socks.

The proverbial stone
in our shoe.

Delaware River in Winter

That Spot By The Tall Oak

I find myself
going back to
the pile of dusty
dirt

just outback at
Mom-mom's house;

that spot
by the
tall oak.

It really looked
deserted and not
quite capable
of holding grass
or giving life
to fallen acorns.

Dusty
dirt,
as
I said.

But,
I played
in it for
hours
on end;

or,
for moments
that seemed

In The Same Place

like
hours
on
end.

And,
that dirt
is
still
in my me.
Today.
Here.
Sticks
planked over
holes
dug with bark
and
broken matchbox
cars caked with
dust
as if
they had
driven—

full-sized—

through the
powdered silt
of memory
and
childhood abandon;

perched
upon imagination
that keeps the
world alive—
and full
of endless possibility.

That Spot By The Tall Oak

Gnarled roots
rising and
falling just
enough
above the
surface to
be shaved
clean by the
pushmower
and time.

I can find
that
place

anytime,

anywhere,
as long
as I may
hold its place
in my me.

Giving me
escape to
a panoply
of mirth
I never knew
I would carry
all this
way

like the
palm full of
dusty dirt
that made me
seem to

In The Same Place

be and rise
to a sense
of sublime
existence
as
a
boy.

That Old Maxwell House Can

The day I could not
wait to see my father
come home so we could
pack up our rods and worms
and head out to the
reservoir—to catch fish
along her banks
felt eternally long in
the waiting.

I must have painted
the low brick wall three
hundred times that day
with the water that
was in that old
Maxwell House can
and my battered old
three inch trim brush
with china bristles.

It was mine to do.
Always as I waited.
Painting and watching
it dry so I could paint it
again and again and again.
On hot days the smell
of drying damp bricks
still gathers in the back
of my nose—forcing
a smile across my face.

When This Place Becomes Everywhere

When time
has passed
enough
and
you
have learned
to milk the marrow
from the
center of
each space
you have built
your life
around;
it will be planted
in
your
cells
in ways
that make you
find it
everywhere
you go.

Where you
stand
will become
so
important
it will lose
all meaning

and
strand

itself
against
itself.

The thing
that means the most
will be empty;
and it shall be
as if everything
and nothing
were yet
the same.
When Jerusalem
becomes an alley,
when Petrograd becomes
a shelter;
heaven will have found
itself on earth,
and the dust
between our
toes will exude
Blake's fearsome
grandeur.

The Pre-Rain Air

The pre-rain air
is heavy-laden

with a dank
moist
mist.

The lingering aroma
of nightcrawlers
and red-shale dirt
rises
among the green
gold banks
of the Delaware
River basin
as the sun
begins its
slow move toward
its setting.

It is no stretch
to close my nose
and smell the
spilled liquid deet
puddled in the
bottom of
our green metal
tackle box—

from
when
I was eight.

The Pre-Rain Air

The deet
wafting up
and mixing with
the aroma of
nightcrawlers and
shale and murky
waters of the
Churchville Reservoir.

As then,
so now.

Carried to my brain
on the follicles
of hair in my nose
for forty-six long
years.

The deet dissolved
the paint and dripped
its way back into my
olfactory networks from
that day forward—I'm
hoping until the day
that I lie down
to die.

It takes no real work
for a nose to reach up
and grab the smells
that rise
above the hugger-mugger
of day to day

and blend with fondness
and lilac contentment;

sweet melancholia

In The Same Place

with amber joy
from over a span
and lifetime lived.

That simple book
I opened just now
took me across the
years to the
libraries of long ago.
Its inside pages
hold the smell
of all the libraries
of all the schools
I attended from 6–14.

I would never have known
by mind
that the smell
was each the same,
but this book—
this book on
The Southern Highlands
gave me sign of
some thing that my
me had no idea
I knew.

Pieces of back there
are strewn around me
everywhere;
here
and
now.

Mincing Words with Whitman

Poems Written at the Grave of Our Native Son
in Camden, NJ

The notions of lineage and evolution are so much a part of who we are as people that they lie beyond the routine and regular layer of life and are hidden below the surface of our explanations. We attach ourselves to people, ideas, notions, things, activities, beliefs, universes and molecules and we are changed because of those connections.

This morning's "chance" meeting with an old friend throws off our schedule and we miss being hit by a truck because we arrived at that intersection fifteen minutes later than we would have if that old friend had not come our way in the morning. The things we attach ourselves to and those that we are attached to change the core of who we are. Our attachments alter us.

We are attached to whole universes. Whole universes are attached to us. From the inception of connection we evolve. These lines themselves get stuck to me and feel—in their sound—as if they were lines from "Leaves of Grass."

Whitman is an attachment of the American people. Like him or not; care for his opus or not you have been changed by the breathing and writing of our true Native Son—Walt Whitman. There is a stickiness to Whitman's style and contribution.

If nothing more than the echo of his free verse on the poetic ethos or his compassionate clarity for helping soldiery amid the Civil War; you are not unscathed. He was right—every atom that was his is ours as well. What he assumed, we assumed—as well. The astro-physicists know this to be true, as does the mystic. So too, does every poet.

Whitman has always been just out there—a little to my right—just beyond reach. I knew I would get to him and the volumes of his worth, just not sure when. It was a few years ago that the very penthos of the words he lodged in our collective being and memory as a people began to condensate in my poetic consciousness and vision.

The "elegiac rants" of Whitman began to make sense. As I gained a voice I felt the prophetic muse walk just out of view—casting a long shadow on my perception and tableaux.

It was a day in the office that thrust this project on me. One too many meetings made me seek the shelter of quiet and subdued growth. I decided to get out of the office for a lunch break and do something to shift the gaze and focus of my day.

NPR had played a brief clip on Whitman that morning and it included a reference to Whitman's house in Camden—just 8 miles west of my desk. I called the Whitman House as I stood at my desk—making an appointment for a tour in ten minutes. It solidified the idea of this project.

Two months later I did the same thing—left the office for a lunch appointment with Whitman. This time, heading to Walt Whitman's grave—only 6.5 miles west of my desk. That is when it hit me. I need to go out for lunch more often. I needed to go to a place of the developing power of word and words.

I would go to lunch at Whitman's grave once a month. I would read a piece of his opus. I would write him an epithetic elegiac rant—a reply to his ethos.

I knew the "Whitman Project" would consume me for a bit. I knew it would captivate me for a considerable amount of time, interest, and passion. It would lure me into Whitman lore, but, also ask my pencil to craft words differently; and, my sensibility to hear speaking in a new way. I mean, how could it not? Here was one big monster poem that Whitman worked and reworked to death over and over spanning the all of his life. One poem; a million renditions. Surely that would change anyone.

* * *

One big sprawling and ambling poem that was crafted and recrafted over time. What a concept. I really did not know that about "Leaves of Grass" until I was in my fifties. Had I missed that in High School English? Did I just forget it?

There is a considerable difference between the first edition of the work and the "death-bed edition." It was worked on and over again and again. At one point, Whitman even glued an addendum into the books when he had finalized his section entitled, "Drum Taps." This add-on was forty three poems about the war. He finished them just after Lincoln's assassination and wanted to get them added to the edition that had just come out prior to the killing.

This sense of fluidity and change is vital in his work. The sense of malleability and process is something that all artists recognize as their craft, but so few go back and rework a thing—almost to death—they just move on.

* * *

I do not think I ever had a sense of how volatile life was for writers in the past. Just the impact of urban fires on the writer in the 1800's was enough to make me pause and praise the idea of data sectoring and sequestration. Drives and ports have saved so many words from a premature death by fire. All those words that have been set free from the page by flame, have never darkened the lintels of the human heart.

That sort of tentativeness to life makes a huge difference in how people live. There is a whole layer of insecurity and risk that we cannot feel. The redundancies of digital living—and that impact on our wholeness—remove some of the impact of the notion that life can be unhinged in a second. We can store things—safely and redundantly—and that leads us to feel a buffer that earlier authors did not know.

I think the transient and unfettered nature of much of Whitman's life allowed him to be a bit more flexible in the rewriting and reworking of Leaves of Grass. He had a high degree of toleration for change and it comes out vividly in his style, content, and approach.

But, then again, so did most of the world's thinkers. Libraries of unduplicated thought were burned to the ground over and over again through history. Lots of the world has burned up and out of our retrievability. It did over and over again in the past. We act as if Alzheimer's is some new blight on the earth. It may be a new predicament for individual humans and their own stores of personal memories, but societies have been wiped clean of memories for most of their time on this earth.

Starting over is something we are having to do less and less. I think it fosters an undue sense of security upon our concepts of time and life. We face this less as authors.

* * *

Whitman wrote novels. I need to get to them, too from his grave. There is no sense seeing only the way he shaped his poems, but the twisting, stretching, and sanding of each and every word he used in its every fashion is vital in making a more complete image of the writer. He also kept extensive journals.

I am moved by his journaling of the crashing of two ships off the shores of his family home in New York. Two separate occurrences left an indelible impression upon his pen. The accidents occurring in the dark of night produced dead bodies on the shore in morning light. Helping to carry and pile the bodies changed him. Feeling he could only wring his hands and gather the bodies of the dead, he had an undone feeling at not being able to keep those dead from death. I believe that changed his sensibilities toward the coming war.

There are infinite streams of craft and sensibility that fed Whitman's poetic vision and work. He was indeed "many" as he mentions in the "Leaves." It is this manifold depth of character that has carried him across the ages as not only innovator of style, but anchor and holder of place in regard to the American experience both then and now.

I dare to mince words with this great weaver of images. I dare to think I have something to say to this formidable giant on the landscape of time and eternity. That which I pen to Whitman is dross against the refined silver and gold of his sentiments, but alas, I need to say these things to him. I need to offer up words to this fellow wordsmith.

Foggy Morning

This Rock Of My Reflection

I have come to find myself
on this rock of my reflection,

Walt,
our NATIVE SON,

just alongside
your resting place—
your burial place.

There is no garland
laurel leaf wreath
here—at this grave—
for you our
greatest troubadour
and bard
of the shifting art.

No fanfare to be sure.

All you will find is
several clumps of hideous,
plastic flowers
left by those who must have
meant well but had no sense
of the beauty
of impermanence and the
impermanence of beauty.

All things fade
and blossom
in a ring of endless
light and hope.

In The Same Place

All things
turn themselves in
upon themselves again
for some sort of nourishment
and sustenance
beyond the grave
that cannot hold them.

This will be my Elegiac Rant;
the dusty dirt gathered and
scattered at my feet amid
the rocks that sleep
with you
in this sullen
repose

almost like a quivering
pause hanging in an eternal
and lifeless space
between time.

This is my cry
across
the surface of life
and
its every limb.

All life hangs here
in this dimension
while you craft
a filigree phrase
with jeweled meaning
and facets of light and glory.

It is your pause.
It is where you
do your work. I sit

in this place of a moistly
laden breeze and
pray a droplet of
your skill
will land on me;
an iota of your respiration
will fill my lungs.
O native son, sing
while I am here

that I may learn the
melody of your leaves.

Those leaves
have been singing
in breezes all over this
fashioned earth of word
and despair.

Sharing The Dirt

I hope
you do not mind
that I have shared
your plot
with others.
Walt.

I have
brought them
to your dirt
that they may
get it caked
on the bottoms
of their shoes,
on the cuffs
of their pants,
in the crackling
hidden places
of their lungs

so that

every atom that
is yours
may
become theirs as well.

Reaching

Reaching out
from my center—

from my me—

is a silent and
ever growing arm;

an implement
of pulling in.

Its hand
is of the essence
of universal grasping,

clutching all the
content and flower
that these my eyes
do see.

Each thing

a seed in the
growing expanse
of evolution and
destruction;

of simplicity and
rebirth.

This goldenrod
a specter
of what will

In The Same Place

be THEN when I
am gone.

I can feel myself
in this vista
of this lake
and this field;
in this place
of space and time—

beyond NOW.

What piece of me
is in this dragonfly
which lights
upon my journal?

Where am I in that
purple flower spread
across the surface
of the lake for
endless acres of
its growing?

My heart
calls out across
the waters to
the reddening leaves
of sassafras and maple;

calls out behind me
to the gurgling creek
and "whipping" whippoorwill
perched

in some old
beech tree invisible
to my eyes.

Reaching

That—
all is me.

This—
all is that.

The Dead

(for Galen)

I have come to
where the dead live
because they have a
fondness for silence
and pauses between
words.

The sloping green
hills of this place
are still enough

are peaceful enough

that the great
blue heron does not
feel a need to leave.
It sits there,
silent
and still—
undisturbed.

Every cubic inch
of this place
seems steeped
in a sacredness
of space
that hallows
what it touches.

This dirt is worthy
of holding our pain.

The Dead

There are bruised
and tender portions
of life that ache
so badly and render
us so paralyzed

that only tears

can be found
on the landscape.

This place makes
that holy.

This is a place
that you could lean
and "loafe" into

at ease

and find yourself
made whole.

Every blade
of grass here
is
formed from this
soil and this air
and leans into
the fabrication of
my soul—of
my being.

Lone Tree

Tanging

I

I listen—
all
the
day
long
for someone
who
is carving out
their words—

crafting them with
simple caring and a
wizened devotion to
perfection in its every
detail.

There is none.

II

I listen
behind
their words,
over
their words, and
under their words for

an inkling

of what might be called
rapture, or glory, or even
a hint of beauty or awe.

In The Same Place

I would settle
for
a
smidgeon
of wonder.

There is none.

III

Pure,
didactic,
opulent,
self-obsession and an
hideous, singularity of despair
is foaming on their
lips; falling to the
ground in piles of
frothy hypocrisy
and un-disguised condemnation
of anyone within range.

It is the way
that words
have come to be

carved out
these days.

Carelessly
with volume
and abandon

high.

IV

There is a habit
to keep bees from swarming

Tanging

a way of breaking

bad news to them.

When a keeper
of hives or skeps
has
died
and
been
laid low
in the ground
for burial and repose,
a loved one
of the keeper

will
slowly approach
to tell the bees
of
the
keeper's
death.

They will utter
softly
in whispered tones
and measured breath
of the loss
and
of the
human desire
for the bees
to stay
and
not
to swarm
beyond the walls

of their present
enclosure
and home
of honeyed sweetness.

V

The hive
will be draped
in black cloth
a covering of wailing
and sympathetic
reaching to hold the bees
in the company of
the grieved.

That one—

that friend of the
keeper—must carve his
words with tenderness
and must craft her words
with longing. It is
how they keep "the place"
in place for the bees—

for the hive.

VI

Death
can move things
and shift things
and make a hive
want to swarm
up and out
of its "here"—

to get away
and leave.

Tanging

Proper crafting
of the words
and carving
of the emotion
are believed
to extend
the pleasantries
of the familiar
and keep the bees

from the swarm
that would carry them
off and away

from their place of living

their place of life.

That skill is lost
here among the living.

There is all
but no unbarbing
of death's sting
for the bee.

It is all but gone
from everywhere
on the horizon
and landscape
of human talk
and speech.
There are almost
none who pause
to hear the sound
of what a word
sounds like

In The Same Place

when it
is carved out
for the hearing
by another.

And that,
that has made
all the difference.

VII

There is a loud
and raucous clanging
of
pots and pans
should the words of
empathetic grief
not meet
the solemn nature of the
moment
and hold the bees
steady
in the place
of their familiar.

This "tanging" is
only for their
swarmed departure
and their
arousal to away—

and none other.
It sets
the world on edge;
it calls,
"there is a leaving,"
that there is "an awaying"
from what has been
to

Tanging

some new thing that
will some day be.

Not before.
Not until.

There is no
preparing
for these times;
no dance
of anticipation
that lets us
know.

There is a swift
and focused
gathering together
of the disparate
portions of the hive
and a leaving
that is upon us in the
twinkling of an eye.

The queen—

in all the warp
and weft

of the stability of
this bonded
and connected
place of unity
and dependence—

is just as likely
to stay as go.

The mitosis

In The Same Place

of this tribe
flashes forth
on what seems
to us
as whim.

Gone.

Let the clanging
of the tanging
begin.

VIII

I long
to hear such words
as would stir in me
a staying beyond the
days of the keeper's death.

Such words as would soothe
some piece of my me in the
change that comes
in the burying of some
large portion of our way
of living and of being. For,
there has been a death,
Walt, to portions of
our being men of
grace and women
of mercy—tenderness
underneath our nails.

I would long to
hear such words
as would be
autumnal and rattle
across the surface of
of our path as humans

seeking to regain our
tender ways of touch.
Those words that
would blow away on
the hint of any small wind—

all dried out
as they could
and
would
be.

Only a sound,
betraying
their departure—
a tanging of the
abandonment of summer
and her long lit lazy days—

will mark
on the instant
when the shift
has come to be.
And the herald
will be a reminder
of what it is we
should be about
and
unwilling to lose
in our flesh.

IX

What men,
Walt,
do so care enough
for the swarming
that they would pause
to craft the communal

In The Same Place

words of reparation with
passion and design?

What women,
Walt,
will make a space
of tenderness and
"together" so inviting
and warm to keep
the hive from having
away.

These are the ones
I listen for; with ears
striving to hear faint strains
and whispers.

My hope is
poised in the longitude
and latitude of grace that
holds out against all odds
for the simple connection
of lips to heart. They
must be moving closer.

Listen.

Is that them?

Bee-Space

There is a space
a bee knows

under three eights
of an inch.

It is
just
enough
space
to move,
and groom,
and feed,

and store.

And,
no more.
And yet,
no more.

Just
enough
and
not so much

as to plaster
and wax against
the forceful wind
and cold, damp
intruders
of the hive—

that carry disease
and death
into the place
of safety.

This space
of dwelling
and recapitulation
is in everything;

we must sense its
edges and go
no
further.

The keeper
hangs his
supers with a
mind to
this space;
knowing
if he is
not aware
and
on the perfect
mark

the bees will
seal him out.

A heart leans into
such a knowledge,
Walt.

A man crafts
his life with
similar
sensibilities.

Bee-Space

Flying from this
field to that
and bringing
home a nectar
for sustaining-through
the hushed
and harsh
cold of winter—

an antidote against
despair.
Seal out
all that is not
in this bee-space
of our own
true self.
The ascetics
knew to guard
the heart.
Diodochos cried
in the desert, "keep
not the door swung
wide on hinge"—

to keep the
heat within.

He measures
space as do
the bees—

over and against
what robs and
kills—a
wounding
invasion.

In The Same Place

And there you
sat, Native Son,

long and long
in the plush
surround
of sound
and deep
musical
drone
of the bees
under your wild
cherry tree.

How it nourished
you and lulled you
into the space
of your heart
where you could meld
the humming of
their song with the
rhapsody of
your sentiment
and
word,
your sensibility
and
image.

This
is
what
wafts itself in
and around
and up out
from
the bee-space
of time and

Bee-Space

lore;

that space of rapture
and whimsy;
rapture and
bucolic symphony.

This loafing
place your bee-space
to guard and
seal; this increment
is your
conscious horizon
of wisdom
and design,
Walt.

Sit
long
and
long
under the
wild-cherry
of your imaginings.
Seal the
heart just
above the measure
of bee-space
that your soulful
gift may not escape.
Let it build
and waft
and foment its
way into our
lives and days.

Love at the Pinnacle

I Speak Gold

I speak green
in the morning
and the day turns
a shade newer—
beyond when I
had spoken brown.

The mind turns
on the hues given
by the meaning
of the day.

The heart turns,
too on the impression
set before it—
dazzled and bejeweled
by the spoken-ness
of a thing and its
palette of interpretation
and display.

In the early morning
pink-en-ing fog

the clouds,

they look
like mountains. They
speak my morning
into an illusory
sense
that gives me pause
to wonder

In The Same Place

what else I may have
misconstrued—one thing

for another.

How ambient
the greening spring

and the slow rusting
movement of time
over the surface
of each leaf;

rippling endlessly
and lithely over mountains'
crenulations and valleys'
sweeping downward pull.

It all moves
toward one end;
it hangs on one
endless yearning.
It awaits that
one day,

when in the morning
I no longer speak
yellows, and oranges,
and reds.

On that day,
that one day
that spans a new and
burgeoning aeon,
I speak gold
into the morning
and every single thing
changes—every thing.

I Speak Gold

Atoms are aglow with
a fire-building translucence
of amber burning yellow.

Ochres of vibrating
scintillators swim
into my soul through
my eyes. I feel
a gladness swell
in me that is
lost between nobility
and mirth. Walking
along the river path
enshrouded in golden
leaves—

a tunnel of light—
boring through
time in an endless
appearance of
the now.
What is a full
surround of
vibrance
eats itself
into my me.

This gold cannot last,
Walt. Robert
told us so. It is
here in earth-time
an hour at most.

But, while here,
it is pulling in gulps
of autumn light

In The Same Place

dragging them to
the ground.

Gulps and gulps of
light line the path
and rattle as I shuffle
my way through them
in rapt conclusion.

This is where the
indolent sun
burns itself
upon the gorgeous
floods of
yellow gold.

I speak gold
and give it voice
in the air
for one
eternal
instant,

for one
eternal
now.
On
more
moment
of the
endlessness
of
golden
LIGHT.

Having to Find Myself

I am having to
find myself;
trying
to remember
who
it was that
stood at my side
only just

this morning—

as we struggled toward
the main of the fighting—

amid the dark,
dreamlike fog
of trying to swim past
the un-sureness in
my soul—
in all our souls and
across every living
thing that is standing
on this our present
battlefield.

You have seen this,
Walt,
a thousand, thousand times
you have seen this
in your ambling wander
through the great
stretches of the war that
we set ourselves to—

In The Same Place

amid the trickling
flood of the chaoses
of the skirmish
and all the mismatch
of impressions and
intentions.

He was a young
man—that I know—
not unlike myself;
but,
his name,
his name is not
close upon my lips—

not anywhere in the air
about the me
that I have become.

He had only just
moved into my tent—
but
a
day ago
or so—

and his name,
his name
I do not know.

He took the bed
of my earlier
friend,

that friend that
only just fell

Having to Find Myself

himself to
his death;
his lonely
solitary death on
the bloody gravel
just beyond
our morning fire.

One day,
a bed belongs
to a friend,
and the next
a stranger finds
his way into it—

a placeholder against
the clouds of purpling,
black powder and lead
of shot.

Walt, O Walt,
peripatetic sage
of these democratic
shores and flowers,
how have you written
this anguish into
parchment with
your pen?

How have you shared
this desperate, ragged, and
suffering condition with the
mothers and the fathers
of the fallen?

We saw you here,
tending
the lads

In The Same Place

who were dying.
We saw you
take to pen
to share a son's
last words with
his ma and with
his pa.

I wonder where
the souls come from
that inhabit all of
these constantly
changing
bodies—

constantly
changing
forms
of God.

Is there some dank
emotion that a land must
feel, that a land
must envelope

at the exact moment
of each death or
whisper of decay;

as the youth which
grew upon it
fall down
in a lifeless heap?
Or does it
pass unnoticed?

Which the worse?
Does some act of love

or whimsy encourage
a dour mood in a man
that marches him
thus off to war—

off toward the grave
when he ages toward
his manhood—

toward his own final
independence?

Is there some
turn of the face—away
from the direction of
the eyes—

that does instill
a calamitous decline
at just that moment?

His step was furtive
and unsure that morning
as we left the campfire.

He turned anxiously
from one side to the
other; looking for some
veiled hint of approval
from those who stood
at his boot—those he
called friend.
Sentinels at his
left and
at his right.

It was that instance of
doubt that made him

In The Same Place

hesitate—
just where
to point his gun,
just where to thrust
his bayonet.

It was then,
Walt,
in that instant
of the instance
of his hesitation
that he fell to the
ground—the ground
on which we both stood—

dead. Just and only
dead.

Write him, Walt,
write them all
an elegy that
will keep us
from doing this
all again—
from doing this
even one more day.

Write him, Walt,
in a way that will help
me remember who
he was and who it
was who took his bed.

For, I am undone
and cannot find
my way.

The Felling of a Tree

Felling a tree is more
than just an episode in
action and making
rugged events come
to pass. It is the
bringing to conclusion
of a neutral set of
eyes upon the land;
a detraction of our
whole and organized being.

It is the closing of
a process of watching
by those who have learned
a way of honoring
and holding dear.
Like the crocuses
of early spring.

The trees standing
on our little piece of
land have memories my
days on earth cannot
share; a depth of knowing
toward which I cannot
compare. Their roots
have pulled up water
that had mingled
with the Lenape and the
trappers that lived on this
soil long before my birth.

Their leaves have taken

In The Same Place

in nutrients from air and
sun that had circulated
in our days of expansion
and rising up out of
the Great Depression.

I have looked—
most often—
not to take the living
trees, but to seek out
for ones long dead.

I have taken them from
their place on the knolls
and in the hollers of
this back piece of land—
by the stream—

the Dry Sawmill Creek.

They have yielded stories
in equal measure to those
yet alive. Their respirations—
in their felling—
are rich, divine talk.
They give their tales
away more freely
in the utter relief of
their falling to the ground.

Somehow
they are set free
from the arduous toil of
pressing on in life
—rugged living—
as my axe and saw
send them
on their final journey.

The Felling of a Tree

I hear them singing as
they are sliced, and chopped,
and burned in my fire—
odes of creation
and destruction;
telling the stories they have
grown into their grain,
and bark, and heartwood;
yarns and tellings
of an historic observation.
Energy abounds in
the completion of
their dying.

Energy is never free;
it only seems to be so
to the uninitiated and young—

them that have not spent enough
to know the ways of one who
has learned to conserve against
the wiles of entropy and time.

There are trees down there—
in the notch of that holler—
that heard the words of Whitman
and Muir. Their flowers
have flourished on the moist,
eternal breath of all great beings;

that they could take on as their
own subtle presence and
tousled respirations.

It has been often—
in my days—
that I have remembered

In the Same Place

my long gone adolescent thoughts
of my own youthful felling
and artful destruction of
the beauty and wonder of
living trees.

It was
a fine black-cherry
of mythic size—
in what is left of the lineaments of
my impressions. We gloried in
the shear size of its trunk.

The first ten or
twelve axe blows set
loose the sullen, primal
aroma that lie gathered
just below the bark.
That smell—rich and robust—
that tangy bite
put us into a frenzy
that we could not have
stopped if we had
dared or wanted to.

I like to think that
I am beyond that
pluck and venom at
this point in my life.

I long to believe
I have resigned those
desires of mastery and
clout to the annals
of what has been spoken
on my life—the history
of what I have done
and become.

The Felling of a Tree

Felling a tree that
has begun its journey
toward becoming soil
has its own lore and
premeditated ken of
saga and storm. If you
leave lay there for a month
or even a year after you
have dropped it, it'll
tell you of inklings and murmurings
as it sprouts ferns and drops pieces
of itself toward the dirt and loam
it has taken as its own trajectory
of becoming and design—

just enough matter laced with
nutrient to make life grow dankly
in its space. O tree,

O comrade of this place among
the hills, and pine, and laurel

won't you give me the grace
to hear the way this earth must grow
into its own replenishment.
Won't you give me warmth and
huddle enclosure of feeling as
I dry my feet and listen
around the fire of your own
burning. I will take
your ashes—slowly—to the

small stand of Moosewood Maples
just beyond my door; and there,

there I will scatter you with an
homage I would pay to the masters.

In The Same Place

O comrade, sylvan brother, you are
among the presence of Whitman
and Muir in your burning; and, you
shall leave a trail of wonder in your
wake. I count your words with
a heart given over to noticing
the rings of your wisdom spread out
upon the surface of our dirt-mother.

The oneness of our atoms will someday
touch again as we set ourselves
toward moments of stardust and
ancient lingering carbons.

Back, always back
to the future
of our golden state
of the garden—where
walking in the cool of
the evening was always,

always a good thing.

Morning on the Delaware

The Time It Takes To Grow A Soul

I

The time it takes
to grow a soul

can vary
on any given day.

Like the crafting
of a poem, some
come full-born into
the light of day
with ease;

others not, take
full coaxing out
of their shadow
to reveal the true
tartan
of the heart.

II

Now I sense
your focused purpose
and measured plan
in growing the
Leaves of Grass
slowly over a
lifetime of expression
and ease. Disentangling
meaning and sound
from the lineaments
of a soul that had felt

The Time It Takes To Grow A Soul

the arrival of a new
way of writing
the heart of a nation.
First this way
and then
that.

III

It may be
accomplished in the
twinkling of an
eye; or it may take
a slow and steady
nurturing—day
in and day out.

A blade of grass
holds the fresh dew
it takes as sustenance;

a river bed
repels this same wetness
away.

IV

We may not know
how the growth will
show itself or how
long it will be around,

spreading itself out
to the far corners of
our understanding and
presence.

Can we measure the
cosmos with a clod of dirt?

In The Same Place

Can we know
tomorrow in a
butterfly's wing?

V

A brown leaf blows
in the wind, sending
its rattle straight

into the heart
through the eyes
and through the ears—
leaving an impression;
changing all it
touches on its
entrance in to the
person.

A calm ripple courses
over the surface
of the imminent self;

a shudder of understanding.

A beacon opens
light out
onto
a vista
that becomes
our way home;

a direction we may not
have made in the dark.

A river takes a bend
by a lolling force that
could free a house—
and all its belongings—

from the moorings
that held it fast only
a moment just before.

A remembrance is
brought to the fore
of the mind;

an old intuition
opens us to the familiar;

and all at once
what was—IS;

in an instant
what is not yet
IS as well.

We can
never know the measure—
one time to the next—

for the bread we bake.

VI

How will we know,

brother of the universe,

when this subtle or
exaggerated change is
about to set itself upon us.

Simple or grand,
the soul is built on
these moments;

and, the moments
in-between
these moments.

The force that enters
our humanness is what
shapes us and the

souls we grow.

From that land—
from that soul-scape—

we become the thing
that we have allowed
all things to make us.

What we allow says
more about our soul-self
then anything we could
pen or say with certainty.

VII

The snow drapes itself
almost endlessly—
somewhat eternally
over the craggy
outcroppings of
red shale and cedar.

I have heard so much
that does not match the
tenor of the reality I see
laced through life all around me.

People point us in a
way they wish us to attend.

We are constantly given only
pieces of what we could
know; what others would
have us to be able to
figure out.

Nature, Walt,
nature does
not discriminate toward
the bias.

A sunflower turns ever so
slightly in the glow of the morning
sun. Now in one place;
and, then in another.

Can it pause or take
itself in a backward glance

toward what it saw yesterday?
Or choose to only take
a portion of the sun's rays
to be its own?

VIII

A memory of a gray
and swelling sea
crosses the horizon
of my me.

Can a borrowed ocean
lead us to an evasive sunset
from an earlier day? Or,
only cascade the shore
with what it chooses
to send?

Is the growing of a soul

In The Same Place

always now; always here;

or, can it be from
the echoes of footfalls

and dust-covered
rose-petals of an earlier

hall we did not
choose to darken?

Alas, who can say?
A moment crashes in on us

and carries us away
to the place of our person
that we are choosing

ourselves to become.
Beauty makes all
the difference.

Where will you
allow yourself to go
to become the "I"
of all becoming, Walt?

What sultry hymn
of our drudgery will
open a place inside
to hear the worth of
the beating heart, Walt?

Can a sparrow leave us
broken to the mysteries of
the sky?

Can a mountain pass freeze

our pride and place us back
in the holler of hallowed simplicity?

IX

It takes the subtle
speech of all we
cannot see; it
takes the intrusive waves
of inkling and of hunch.

The dead, Walt,
the dead know for sure.

Whisper the words
into the sunrise for us;

scatter the meaning in the
desert sands.

Without the dead we would
be sore pressed to know.

The time it takes to grow a soul
is now, the place
it takes to grow
a soul is here;

and yet it cannot
only be just now
and here.

It must also hold
a numinous hand
out toward the fading
"then" and allusive "there."

What was,
and is,

In The Same Place

and
is to yet
become

are woven
seamlessly and
unbeknownst
into the
tartan of our days.

A soul is grown
in this way,

a me becomes itself.

A Settling Mist

(for Glinda, Zachary, Josiah)

Outside—
a settling mist
falls so familiar
and so fair.

It is an imperceptible
blanket of content
morning rapture and
warm glow release
that holds me in

this place as if
melted in my own
bed at home—with
Glinda; the boys
moving slowly
in their rooms
to greet the day.

It is here—
with a book
of simple words
and a cup of
coffee—I am
able to bring that
outside air and
bliss inside myself
to grow.

In The Same Place

It is a full surround
gift of words and
notions—

slowly
trickling over the
rocks of mystery
and manner that
pulsate out from
the timeless beyond
and back.

This day
holds no special
claim on the life
that moves within
this sack of cells;

it is the scintillating
strand of poetry
that impresses itself
in me and back—

always back—
through time to

all their hearts
and pens. It is not
just Bly, and Hass,
Shihab-Nye, Snyder,
and Stafford
that glow; it is Frost

and Whitman, Shelley,
and Satho, Basho,
and Issa—the

whole damned lineage

of word craft sorters
and impression laced
builders that shatter my
isolation with light.

Light creeps in slowly
and replaces my me
with a they that falls
lusciously over the

rocks of time and
sings a melody of
infinite meaning and
a camaraderie of
of all that unites

us beyond our skin.

Having to Amble

I am having
to amble my way
slowly,
slowly along
the river;

padding my way
through the disinterested
fog as it rolls and
blows about.

There is a shrouding
blindness that comes
with this clouding mist;

hiding mostly all
that should be in my
line of sight.

Where has it all
gone? What has
befallen the earth
I knew? Will it
emerge again at the
decimation of
this dragon's breath?

There is a keen
likeness
in this
to my days
in midlife.

Rendered unfamiliar
with terrain I so
desperately long
to remember; I plod
on hoping—always
hoping that my next

step will open my eyes;
that my next bend in
the road will make everything
once again clear.

Old Barn Near Pt. Pleasant

I Am Not Sure

I am not sure
how it will be for
us, Walt, in
mid-century when
the temperature rises
nine degrees; how
it will be for them.

The ones we
leave our dying
leaves of grass.

I am sure
you are aware
of how important things
have become. Numbers
especially. How 350
is the safe number
of parts per million
that we can release
of carbon. How nine
is way too hot to
keep the mammoth glaciers
alive on this one planet.
How we passed the
inner markers of our
greed years ago before
we knew they were heralds
of doom, not the dawn.

We have lost our
desire to amble
as a species;

In The Same Place

amble out under the
stars, between the groves,
among the rivulets and
hollers filled with cold
air and gentle winds.
We prefer our houses
to the wild; we would
rather our devices
than a fire.

I had a glimpse—be it
ever so swift—of a leaf
turned over by that
odd wind just before a
storm. The one that
lifts a leaf up, and over
on to its back. I felt the
cold air drop in
just before the storm
hit with thunder
and a mighty
gale.

Then I thought,
perhaps
it is best we
do not live more often
in the wilds. Perhaps it
best we do not custom
ourselves to ambling
strolls among the beauty
of the simple and
untouched woods. It
will be less of a
disappointment and a shock
when all nature unravels
before our very eyes.

The oceans, Walt,
are filling up with acid.
We have burned too
much coal and gas.
It gets trapped in
the new rains and
falls back to our earth
dissolving calcium
where ever it
is found. The shells
of mollusks, and oysters,
clams and mussels cannot
bear the loss to their
skeletal homes much
more. They crumble in
the sand on which
they lay. The coral
itself just disappears.
We have learned
to undo that which
has take aeons to
find its way into
living. We have
learned to do it
and not to care.
How should we
find our way into
the future;
I
am
not
sure.

The Ambivalence Of A Cloud

The ambivalence
of a cloud that has
no concern for cadence
and rhyme or even
sound itself.
It just lolls through
the unaffected heavens
never tasting our
anguish and pain.

Bravo, cloud!

The Way Of Waiting

There is a way
to waiting; a path
through space and
time which one
embarks upon
with little
conscious thought.
It is uniquely
yours and no
one else's

exactly.

It's how you
hold yourself in
the want and yearning
of what is not yet—
what has yet to
come to be.

It is the
texture of what you
allow yourself
to feel, and think,
and do amid the
not yet arrived.

Snowdrops
pushing
up and out,
through the
snow.

I Find It Fitting

I find it fitting,
Walt, that a hawk
sits sentinel above
the dust you
have become—the
dirt we all bequeath
to them above.
It screams enough
to let you know
that I have come
to sit, to loaf, to lean
into the day,
the very day itself.

On this spectacular
of summer days,
the granite blocks strewn
about your grave are
the only seats a man
can find to sit his soul
down to mull, and muse
and ponder the sufferings
of this life.

No church is unlocked,
not one temple is unbarred.
No amphitheater left open
save the truest Coliseum—

where everything sits out
under this marvelous sky.

How is it that we have

wedeled contemplative
loafing out of our human
agenda and desire?
It is a sadder day
for sure. How have we
seen it fit to order
every moment
of our days with
an endless list of tasks? It
is untamable at best.
An orderly thicket,
to be sure.

It is grand
that we have not—
as of yet—learned
how to keep
the messy acorns from
falling. It is glorious
that the weeds have
learned to mock us
with their tenacious
gift of towardness
and "life-ing."
Without
our
permission.

Some things will out
even if we prey
on them and seek the
desolation of their being.

But here, sitting
where no man or woman
has a vote, where no
quorum is possible at all;
here, where no take-over

In The Same Place

or no buy-out approaches
the lips of those planted
here in this soil—them
that abide here
there is a sane stillness.
Here,
my hope is once again
given wing that the
madness of our human
ego will one day rest.
One day a calm
will prevail. Oh,
that men would taste
it before the ground.
Oh, that women would
touch it before
the grave.

It is here,
in this present
instant and ancient
hunger to learn
and loaf and love the
"allness" of all there is.
It is here.

Old Barn Near Pt. Pleasant

The Climate March Poem—A Rant

I—My Bare Foot

I placed my
bare foot firmly
on the soil
of a planet that
longs for the
thinking ones
to think;

that yearns for
the clever ones
to wake up,

and

take action
beyond their simple
speech.
That they
act as the noble
woman upon
which they all stand
and drill
and offer up the
remnants of all they
have taken
from her
and destroyed.

Her ancient plates
and seismic shifts
move not on a

The Climate March Poem—A Rant

whim or
self involved
reflection of profit—

as does their
every move.

No market share
or stock options
are hers to garner
from her constant
attention
to the landscape
all about her and
within—
as are theirs.

She is shaped
and pressed by
the forces of
all that touch
her. And in
that touch
she always attempts
to bring a balance
that is beyond
any one member
of her system
of life and living.

Whole planets spin
through space
completely unaffected
by the greed of
what we have built
here on our place
with our singular
focus and vision

In The Same Place

on our own
lives—

lives
that are willing
to offer everything
else up on the
altars of destruction,
extinction, and
a consumption
that knows no
satiation.

And yet,
with the Buddha
we hold up
one
simple
flower
that all mankind
would become
awakened before
they fossil fuel
themselves to
death.

The Climate March Poem—A Rant

II—Burning All His Trees

How could we live
with ourselves if
the storms grew
worse for our children
and we did nothing
to bridle our apathy
and our greed.

A blanket cloud
of methane cannot
replace a cumulus.
A river
of polychlorinated biphenyls
cannot replace a spring.

We could loaf and
lean and
invite ourselves no more
to quench our deepest cataracts
on the cold, cold draught
of our hydration.

Like all the earth
a composite of water and dirt.

How could we live
knowing the stones we
gave our children—

as the asked for bread—

In The Same Place

fell on them and
crushed them dead
or, at least impaired
them—no more to
lean and loaf with Whitman?

The rocks have not
yet joined the cry of
dissidence and revolt;
the stones have not yet
thrown themselves
on the barons
and corporate moguls
whose tales and lies
have lolled us away
from finding the
trail to their pockets
well-lined with cash
and misinformation.

If a man knew
that burning all his trees
would kill the children
of his home,
would he not look
for a new way to heat
the rooms of his sons—
to light the rooms
of his daughters?

Could he knowingly
march toward the cliff
of his lemming demise with
no concern for the falling
save his own?

The shadow play
of rain upon the bark

The Climate March Poem—A Rant

has given me hope
a thousand, thousand times.
The muffling stillness
of foot on loam
has caused me
endless pause to
listen beyond myself.
But others,
will they wake
in time?

I do not know,
I do not know.

The Climate March Poem—A Rant

III—A Canyon of Woe

A canyon of woe
could not replace
the loamy soil
of home.

And yet, each day
I see the tracks
upon the land
that will surely
shatter the dank
and fertile coordinate
of our hope.

The moist dirt
below our feet.

I feel the trails
and hills in the
center of my me,
a tonic against
the mid-day
toil and focus on
my madly hauling
cash and acquisition—
a wall of ennui to
protect the bounty
of my greed.

How might we
then cope,
should we toxify the

The Climate March Poem—A Rant

very respite of our
toxification?

And, that sound
has no easy listening.
The words of a
dying earth do not
so easily find
themselves in verse.

It is not for the simple rhyming
that they are kept from being
penned.

Toxification.

It's very harshness cuts
words in two; lacerating one
good image upon the altar
of our poetic druidry and one
good sound upon the misty
morning grass of my
Glencoe prose.

Craning my neck to
assail my eyes with
the wonder of a mountain
climb, I know the
stakes of endlessly fossil
fueling ourselves to the
edge. We will fall—
as all tipping points—
in a whispered descent that
picks up speed.

Unrecognizable
at first. But,
oh too soon upon us, still.
Unless,

unless we make
the ultimate
of all noble sacrifices—

to make a choice to
bridle our rampant
greed for our singular
need to have and use
and devour every
living resource
at our surround.
To begin to say
"NO" to living
in a flippant
ease and
decadent superiority—
numb to the
languishing
and suffering
of every other being that
draws breath.
Me,
my,
glorious and
singularly infatuated
with its own
ownness so much
it pretends
that
there
is
NOTHING
ELSE.

And soon,
as it also dies,
it will briefly
become
true.

From Penn's Sylvan Lands

(Written for the inauguration of Governor Tom Wolf)

It had to have
been early, that he
walked gently
the leaf covered
ground—marsh marigolds
and snowdrops sharing
an infrequent bed
along the water they
had come to know as
home. The Delaware
shared the only space
they had known
with a man and a
people they did not;

no smell of
phosphates then
in her waters
that lap to this day
on the moss covered
rocks—greenish gold
in the sunlit afternoon.

The moist smell
of loam under leaf
kicked up from every
step and filled
a man with lineaments
and latitudes of his
covalent bond with and
to the land. The canopy—

In the Same Place

a roof to tuberous growths
of "sang" and stretching
limbs of sassafras that
golden-ed in the
autumn letting go
of green—was a sheltering
home for deer and bear;
berries and roots, fox and
otters. Today, most know
these things as
myth or photos from
a book or label
of their consuming.
How long, just
how long can a man—
any man—stand upon
the very earth he digs
out from under? Would we
not ridicule a man like that?

How much would
it cost for us to learn
to migrate compassion from
the leaking extraction pipes
of the soul of man? Could the
seepage of understanding and
deliberation poison the waters
of the planet's skin to a positive
detriment? As crazy as this
sounds to most, should we
not be wincing at the reality
of the fracking well?

This rock has
been here too long
for me to imagine
its beginning. These
Appalachians have cut

From Penn's Sylvan Lands

our home in two and
risen to fall again under the
weathered weight of erosion
and tectonic debris. Billions of
years of measured change
have made and destroyed a
landscape with only wonder
as its ravishing by-product
and disease. This earth
longs for the audacity of
such a man as could leave
only awe in his wake, tender
blossoms of the Spring Beauty
under the fall of each footstep.

The earth has a way of
destroying into beauty; of
decaying into rapture. Erosion
takes what it must
to the bottoms
of the hills for
the furtive streams to
carry to the daffodils nestled
along the winding, lacy
watershed. The half-life
of a fallen tree is
seditiously displaced
by nutrients and the
alluviation of all sorts
of earth debris that
piles on over windblown
time and buries what is there
to amass pockets of oil and coal
and sediment for the great
day of mountain making
and geologic shifts of
newly discovered tectonic plates.
Our power needs are a

In The Same Place

crumb to the monstrous
mountain passion movement
of the lithosphere; our toxic greed
is laughed at by the ability of
life to destroy and remain.
Would that a man
would arise that took his
place to steer us in
a gentle communion
with the music of the spheres, with the
cresting of metamorphic creation,
and the undertow of natural decay.

Sing, Blue Mountain of the rain
carried across your face to the
the tributaries and the waters of
our Delaware. Sing, Hawk Mountain
of the feathers cutting wind across
the tree tops on your soil, mid-air
on their dancing flight of
mating and migration.
Sing, Susquehanna
as the shallows gurgle slowly
over stone at the bottom of
ridges formed in Alleghenian
orogeny. Sing, land
of ancient rivers of
the world; sing, land
of ancient mountains. Call
for the coming of a people
that know the beauty of what
they have. Call for the coming
of leaders who lead toward
healing. When the Ravens
cry at the capital and are fed, when
deer find grass among the Outlets,
then will we have found a peace
with the dirt on which we stand.

From Penn's Sylvan Lands

The dirt from which
we are composed and
do so quickly return.

How long, just
how long can a man—
any man—stand upon
the very earth he digs
out from under? Would we
not ridicule a man like that?

It had to have
been early, that he
walked gently
the leaf covered
ground—marsh marigolds
and snowdrops sharing
an infrequent bed
along the water they
had come to know as
home. The Delaware
shared the only space
they had known
with a man and a
people they did not;

no smell of
phosphates then
in her waters
that lap to this day
on the moss covered
rocks—greenish gold
in the sunlit afternoon.

The moist smell
of loam under leaf
kicked up from every
step and filled

In the Same Place

a man with lineaments
and latitudes of his
covalent bond with and
to the land. The canopy—
a roof to tuberous growths
of "sang" and stretching
limbs of sassafras that
golden-ed in the
autumn letting go
of green—was a sheltering
home for deer and bear;
berries and roots, fox and
otters. Sing again
eagle, sing again hawk.
Drown out the gasping
of our greed.

Bring us back
to ourselves

we are not
so far gone

that we cannot
return.

Bring us back
to ourselves.

Upon This Brittle Soil

Walt, we had no idea
of the speed at which
we were making our planet
come undone. We forgot
that each piece is
somehow inextricably woven in
and bound to the whole.
We realized—too late—
our hunger for progress was
somehow making the
earth brittle right under
our own standing. We
were undermining our
very position in life
to live and to continue
to offer life to our
children and their
children as well.

Sing with me the song
of convenience and ease
that we have written on
our souls these last eighty
years. Sing with me the
song of extracted things
that we have taken for
ourselves and away from
others. Sing with me how
we could not stop
ourselves from grabbing
more and more and still
more; unable to stop
ourselves if we had

In The Same Place

even wanted.

When you sat there,
beside the dying lad—

knowing all was lost for
him—did you get a sense that
the bigger world had somehow
changed? Did you feel
that we had crossed some
devastating line when we
allowed this thing
to be loosed on the soil
of our democratic experiment
for freedom and self-determination?
Could we have changed
the day we felt it
kind and true to kill our
brothers in that great
war upon our soil?
The day we felt it
noble to hold a
man as slave?

Whenever?!

We have now become
slaves
of our own
hideous
unbridled-ness
and rampant,
unrestrained freedom.

Ignoble, but a
natural end
to a greed that
knows no "no."

Overgrown

O Camden, My Camden

O Camden, my Camden,
how the years have
held you down and
kept you from the
mighty growth you
knew before so well.

Your noble majesty
and steady invincibility
are gone on the lacquered
decking of the last
ship to be built
on the murky shores
of your Del-a-ware.

Nine square miles now
stand in a deep and
epic want; unable
to be more than
the nation's
lowest rung of poverty
and highest rung of crime—

in the eyes of
oh so many.

How has this sad
oppression
reared its manifold
and ugly heads?

Why does
mankind test

O Camden, My Camden

its ability to choke
the better angels
of our nature;
crushing
the diamond
souls
of our brothers
into dust that
is trampled
underfoot?

O Camden, my Camden,
where is the longitude
of our once-held greatness?
How have we misplaced
the latitude of
Whitman's "City of Friends"?

A child cries
into endless space—
hungry and poor;
a young man
bleeds into
the cavernous abyss—
shot by a friend.

O Camden, my Camden,
how lost the spirit
of ingenuity; and, how
discovered the textures
of decay. Doorframes
burnt and fallen; lintels
cracked and crumbled
barring entrance and
escape. How once we
stood upon these stoops
in pride. How once our frame
and stature stood so tall.

In The Same Place

And still, the city
teems with endless
neighborhoods of love
that long to have
the resources to
rebuild. Neighbor stands
with neighbor and asks
for a day to become
great again.

Who will
break the shackles of
urban pain?

Who cares these days;
who cares to raise the hope
of even one of Camden's
youth? Who dares these
days; who dares to knock
down the barriers of
inequality and despair?

O Camden, my Camden,
what language shall I use
to bring attention to
the barrenness of your
corners? What paint could
I mix in ochre shades
and colors to brush
attention into council
chambers and human
rights debates?

I would plant you
full of trees again;
and, build bee hives
throughout your streets;

O Camden, My Camden

that a greening would
feed the eyes of promise
and that innovation would
pollinate your future days.

May trees line
your corridors of
commerce, may pollen
color the dancing
in your streets and
honey sweeten all
the hearts of those that
are marking a day
of a new invincibility.

O Camden, my Camden,
how we must recreate and
walk the river path together,
pounding tenderness and
human kindness back into
our soil and back into
the bottom-line of
corporate expansion and
incentives.

The eyes
of so many
look up to see the day
when their lives
will be raised up and
out of the shadow of what this
City has become.

ALL of your greatness—
ALL OF IT—
is in the eyes of your
children. They long to

weave their tears together
into a tapestry of loving
warmth and comfort.

O Camden, my Camden,
it is time we let go of the
disparate pieces of ourselves
and lean into and invest
in the joyful good that is
rising from our soil;
from our hearts. Plant
praise in the ears of all
the young. Establish
resources for the houses of
faith. Fill schools with
art and an intoxicatingly
innovative revolutions
of the mind. Show support
for programs of promise.
Water the souls of those
parched in good doing.

Find them, find all of
the children who bring love
down on this City and
let them breathe—even if for
one moment—a sigh that says
they know they will rise up;

they know they have been heard;
they know that they are loved.

O Camden, my Camden,
we are not enemies here,
gathered together on this
small nine miles of soil.

We must set all men to

O Camden, My Camden

be **friends**. We must strengthen
our **bonds of affection**. We must
let swell the **mystic chords** of
our memory. We must let rise
the jobs upon our shores.

I will stand atop what
already exists here as a
City of Friends. I will fight
the **attacks** of the rest.
I will establish—in me—
that **quality of robust love**,
that it may seep every crevice
of this garden of life and make
it **invincible** again. It shall
be more than just a dream,
you dreamed, Walt. I will
learn to make it so. WE will
learn to make it so.

O Camden, my Camden
be born anew on the dust
of words from Lincoln's
mouth and Whitman's
pen—and all we have
come to know
since then—
to be true.

Let not the past
have come to be
in vain. Look for the
fragile infant bird
of change to rise
up from the ashes of
our discontent and the
dust of their very words.

In The Same Place

"But, in a larger sense, we can not dedicate — we can not consecrate — we can not hallow — this ground. The brave men, living and dead, who struggled here, have consecrated it, far above our poor power to add or detract. The world will little note, nor long remember what we say here, but it can never forget what they did here. It is for us the living, rather, to be dedicated here to the unfinished work which they who fought here have thus far so nobly advanced. It is rather for us to be here dedicated to the great task remaining before us — that from these honored dead we take increased devotion to that cause for which they gave the last full measure of devotion — that we here highly resolve that these dead shall not have died in vain — that this nation, under God, shall have a new birth of freedom — and that government of the people, by the people, for the people, shall not perish from the earth."

Abraham Lincoln
The Gettysburg Address
November 19, 1863

"I DREAM'D in a dream, I saw a city invincible to the
    attacks of the whole of the rest of the earth;
I dream'd that was the new City of Friends;
Nothing was greater there than the quality of robust
    love—it led the rest;
It was seen every hour in the actions of the men of
    that city,
And in all their looks and words."

Walt Whitman
"I Dreamed In a Dream," *Leaves of Grass*